LEXINGTON PUBLIC LIBRARY

D1271608

WOMEN
LEADING
THE WAY

Jill Biden

Educator

by Elizabeth Neuenfeldt

BLASTOFF!
2
READERS

BELLWETHER MEDIA • MINNEAPOLIS, MN

Blastoff! Readers are carefully developed by literacy experts to build reading stamina and move students toward fluency by combining standards-based content with developmentally appropriate text.

 Level 1 provides the most support through repetition of high-frequency words, light text, predictable sentence patterns, and strong visual support.

 Level 2 offers early readers a bit more challenge through varied sentences, increased text load, and text-supportive special features.

 Level 3 advances early-fluent readers toward fluency through increased text load, less reliance on photos, advancing concepts, longer sentences, and more complex special features.

★ **Blastoff! Universe**

Reading Level

BLASTOFF! Beginners — Grade **K**

BLASTOFF! READERS — Grades **1–3**

BLASTOFF! DISCOVERY — Grade **4**

This edition first published in 2022 by Bellwether Media, Inc.

No part of this publication may be reproduced in whole or in part without written permission of the publisher. For information regarding permission, write to Bellwether Media, Inc., Attention: Permissions Department, 6012 Blue Circle Drive, Minnetonka, MN 55343.

Library of Congress Cataloging-in-Publication Data

Names: Neuenfeldt, Elizabeth, author.
Title: Jill Biden : educator / by Elizabeth Neuenfeldt.
Description: Minneapolis, MN : Bellwether Media, 2022. | Series: Blastoff! Readers: Women Leading the Way | Includes bibliographical references and index. | Audience: Ages 5-8 | Audience: Grades K-3 | Summary: "Relevant images match informative text in this introduction to Jill Biden. Intended for students in kindergarten through third grade"– Provided by publisher.
Identifiers: LCCN 2021041244 (print) | LCCN 2021041245 (ebook) | ISBN 9781644875940 (library binding) | ISBN 9781648346699 (paperback) | ISBN 9781648346057 (ebook)
Subjects: LCSH: Biden, Jill–Juvenile literature. | Educators–United States–Biography–Juvenile literature. | Presidents' spouses–United States–Biography–Juvenile literature.
Classification: LCC E918.B53 N48 2022 (print) | LCC E918.B53 (ebook) | DDC 973.934092 [B]–dc23
LC record available at https://lccn.loc.gov/2021041244
LC ebook record available at https://lccn.loc.gov/2021041245

Text copyright © 2022 by Bellwether Media, Inc. BLASTOFF! READERS and associated logos are trademarks and/or registered trademarks of Bellwether Media, Inc.

Editor: Betsy Rathburn   Designer: Gabriel Hilger

Printed in the United States of America, North Mankato, MN.

Table of Contents

Who Is Jill Biden?

Jill Biden is an author and educator. She is also a First Lady of the United States!

Jill wants to help people learn.

5

Pennsylvania State
Capitol building

Jill was born on June 3, 1951.
She grew up in Pennsylvania.

Young Jill was a leader.
She often helped
her classmates.

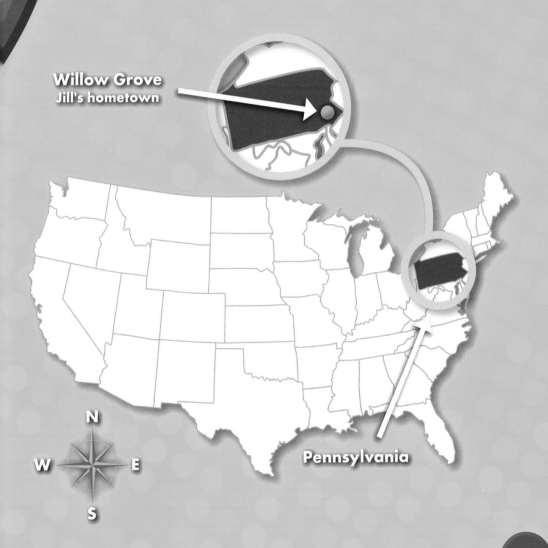

Willow Grove
Jill's hometown

Pennsylvania

N
W E
S

Getting Her Start

Jill studied English in college. She became a teacher.

Jill kept learning. She earned two master's **degrees**.

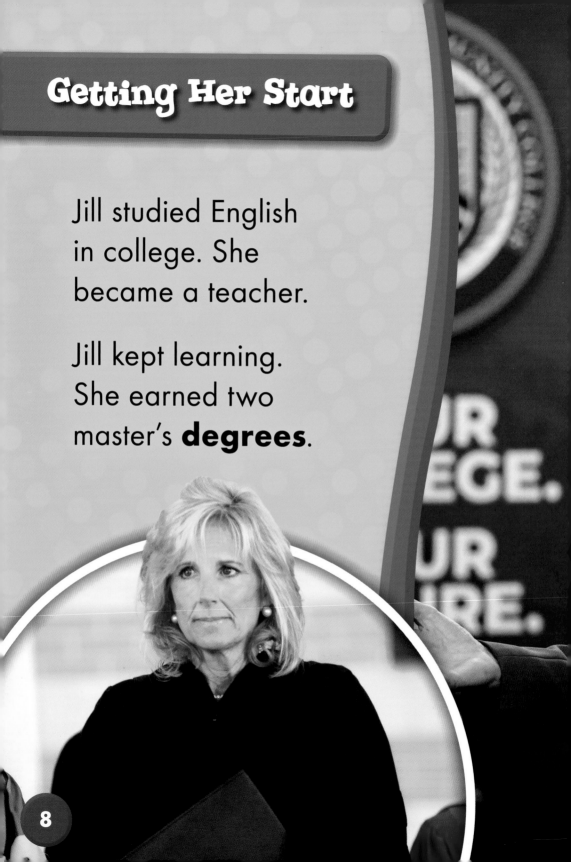

"TEACHING IS NOT
WHAT I DO.
IT'S WHO I AM."
(2020)

Jill married Joe Biden in 1977. They were very busy. Joe was a **senator**. Jill taught high school and college students.

Jill and Joe Biden in 1987

Jill Biden Profile

Birthday: June 3, 1951

Hometown: Willow Grove, Pennsylvania

Field: education

Schooling: studied English and education

Influences:
- her students

She earned a **doctorate** in education in 2007.

Changing the World

In 2009, Joe became vice president of the U.S. Jill became the Second Lady!

As Second Lady, Jill **advocated** for **community colleges**.

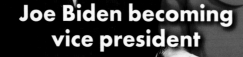

Joe Biden becoming vice president

"EDUCATION DOESN'T JUST MAKE US SMARTER. IT MAKES US WHOLE." (2018)

Jill and Joe's
son, Beau

Jill and Joe's son passed away
in 2015. He had **cancer**.

Jill and Joe formed a program to help cancer **research**.

In 2020, Jill helped
Joe run for president.
She spoke at many events.

Text UNITED To 30330

BID=N

PRESIDENT

Joe becoming
president

Joe won! Jill became
the First Lady.

Jill's Future

Jill visiting with the National Guard

As First Lady, Jill wants to make colleges more **affordable**.

She also plans to help military families.

Jill Biden Timeline

2009	**Jill becomes the Second Lady of the United States**
2010	**Jill hosts the first White House Summit on Community Colleges**
2012	**Jill writes her first children's book, *Don't Forget, God Bless Our Troops***
2017	**Jill and Joe form the Biden Cancer Initiative and Beau Biden Cancer Moonshot to fight cancer**
2021	**Jill becomes the First Lady of the United States**

Jill is still a teacher. She continues to **inspire** her students.

She wants everyone to have **access** to education!

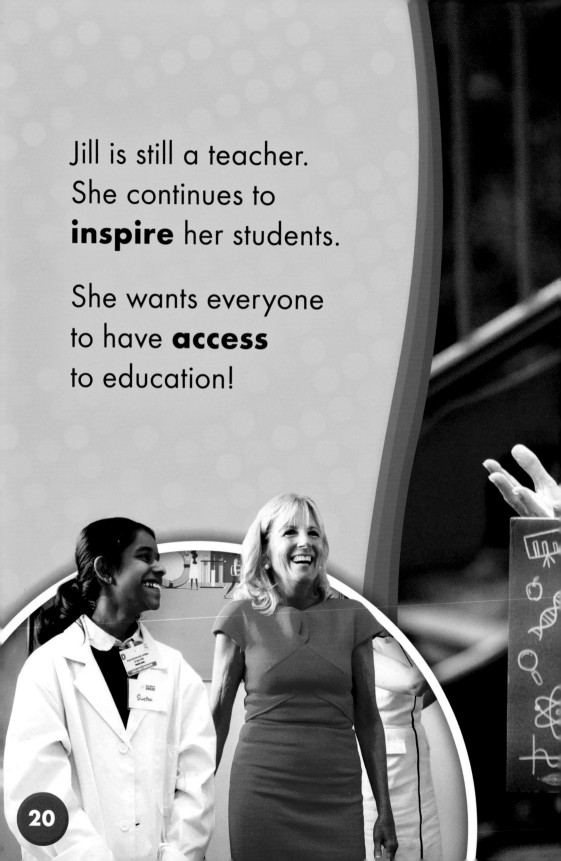

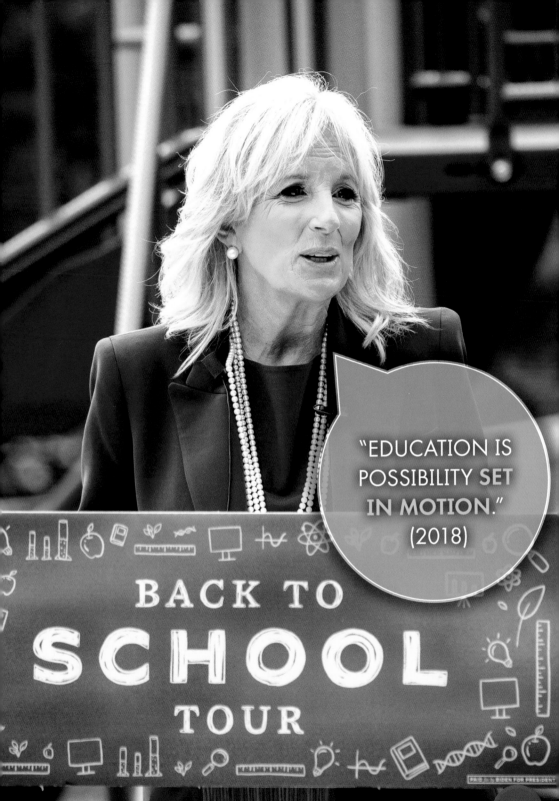

"EDUCATION IS POSSIBILITY SET IN MOTION." (2018)

BACK TO SCHOOL TOUR

Glossary

access—the ability to use or get something

advocated—supported and argued for a cause

affordable—within someone's ability to pay

cancer—a serious disease caused by cells that are not normal and that can spread to different parts of the body

community colleges—two-year schools that are supported by the government and offer an associate's degree

degrees—titles given by colleges or universities

doctorate—the highest degree that is given by a university

inspire—to give someone an idea about what to do or create

research—the information collected on a subject

senator—a member of the Senate, a group that forms part of the United States Congress; it is a senator's job to make laws for the United States.

To Learn More

AT THE LIBRARY

Andrews, Elizabeth. *Jill Biden: Educator & First Lady of the United States*. Minneapolis, Minn.: Abdo Kids, 2022.

Monroe, Alex. *Joe Biden*. Minneapolis, Minn.: Bellwether Media, 2022.

Neuenfeldt, Elizabeth. *Kamala Harris: Vice President*. Minneapolis, Minn.: Bellwether Media, 2022.

ON THE WEB

FACTSURFER

Factsurfer.com gives you a safe, fun way to find more information.

1. Go to www.factsurfer.com.

2. Enter "Jill Biden" into the search box and click 🔍.

3. Select your book cover to see a list of related content.

Index

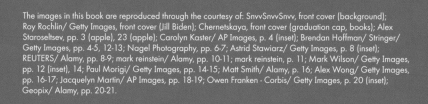
The images in this book are reproduced through the courtesy of: SnvvSnvvSnvv, front cover (background);
Roy Rochlin/ Getty Images, front cover (Jill Biden); Chernetskaya, front cover (graduation cap, books); Alex
Staroseltsev, pp. 3 (apple), 23 (apple); Carolyn Kaster/ AP Images, p. 4 (inset); Brendan Hoffman/ Stringer/
Getty Images, pp. 4-5, 12-13; Nagel Photography, pp. 6-7; Astrid Stawiarz/ Getty Images, p. 8 (inset);
REUTERS/ Alamy, pp. 8-9; mark reinstein/ Alamy, pp. 10-11; mark reinstein, p. 11; Mark Wilson/ Getty Images,
pp. 12 (inset), 14; Paul Morigi/ Getty Images, pp. 14-15; Matt Smith/ Alamy, p. 16; Alex Wong/ Getty Images,
pp. 16-17; Jacquelyn Martin/ AP Images, pp. 18-19; Owen Franken - Corbis/ Getty Images, p. 20 (inset);
Geopix/ Alamy, pp. 20-21.